THE CYRUS CHESTNUT
COLLECTION

T0052804

CONTENTS

Cover Photo: Roy Zipstein

ISBN 0-634-00112-4

HAL•LEONARD®
CORPORATION
7777 W. BLUEMOUND RD. P.O. BOX 13819 MILWAUKEE, WI 53213

Visit Hal Leonard Online at
www.halleonard.com

BIOGRAPHY

Cyrus Chestnut was born in Baltimore, Maryland on January 17, 1963. He first received piano lessons from his father, McDonald Chestnut. He first played publicly at church at the age of seven.

Cyrus attended the Peabody Preparatory Conservatory, obtaining a certificate in piano and music theory. From 1981-85 he attended Berklee College of Music in Boston, graduating with a degree in jazz composition and arranging.

Between 1986 and 1991, Cyrus played and recorded with groups led by Jon Hendricks, Terence Blanchard, Donald Harrison, and Wynton Marsalis. In 1991, he became Betty Carter's pianist.

His career as a leader began with a self-produced Gospel album *There's a Brighter Day Comin'*. He then made three albums for the Japanese label Alfa: *The Nutman Speaks*, *The Nutman Speaks Again*, and *Another Direction*. All were received with acclaim worldwide, with *Another Direction* receiving the Golden award by the prestigious Japanese magazine *Swing Journal*. In 1994, Chestnut became an exclusive Atlantic recording artist, with seven albums in release as of this writing.

Although the listener can clearly hear his gospel roots, Cyrus Chestnut shows a deep knowledge of the history of jazz piano in his performances, ranging from the sounds of Art Tatum, Tommy Flanagan, Hank Jones, and Red Garland. He has an eclectic yet lyrical style, romantic yet fun at the same time.

DISCOGRAPHY

Blue Skies, My Funny Valentine – Another Direction – Evidence 22135

Caravan, Elegie, Tenderly – Nut – Evidence 22152

East of the Sun (And West of the Moon) – Earth Stories – Atlantic 82876

Revelation – Revelation – Atlantic 82518

Note: Recordings released on the Evidence label were originally recorded for the Japanese label Alfa Jazz.

East of the Sun

(And West of the Moon)

Words and Music by Brooks Bowman

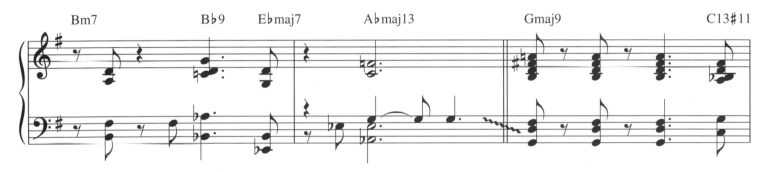

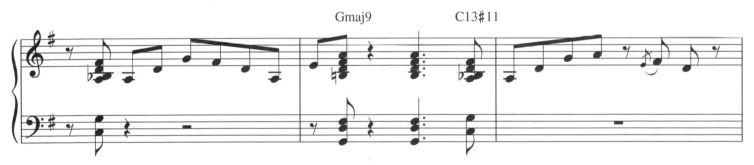

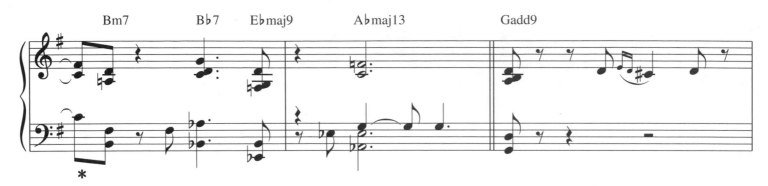

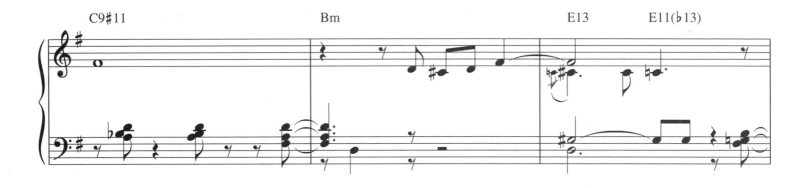

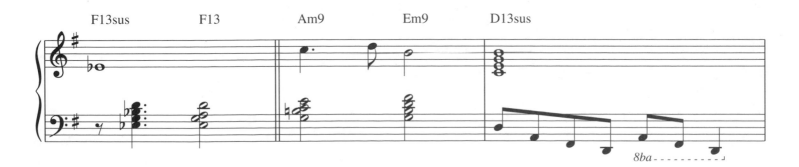

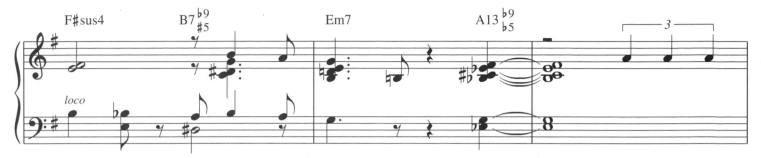

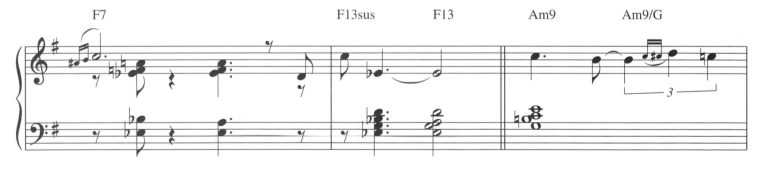

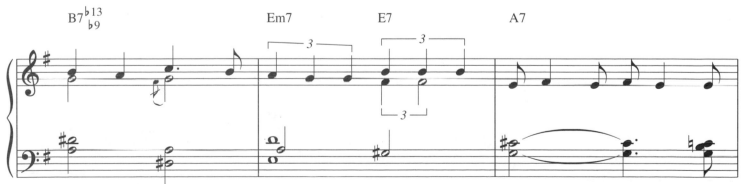

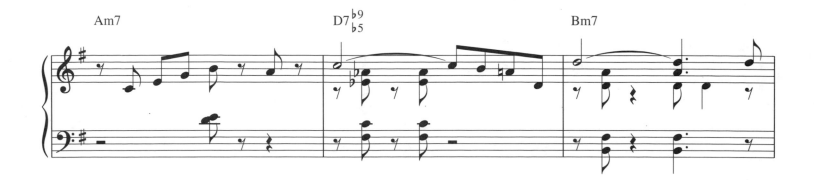

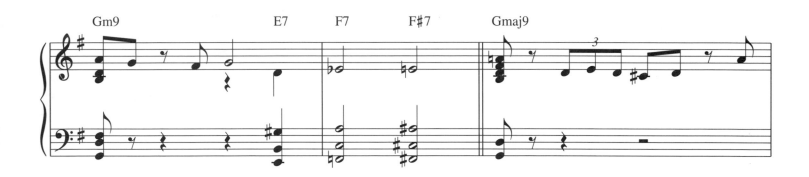

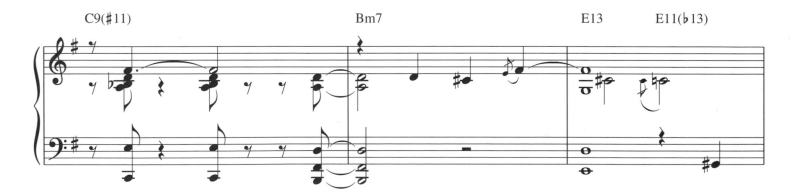

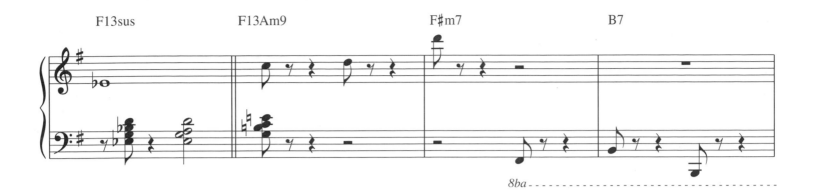

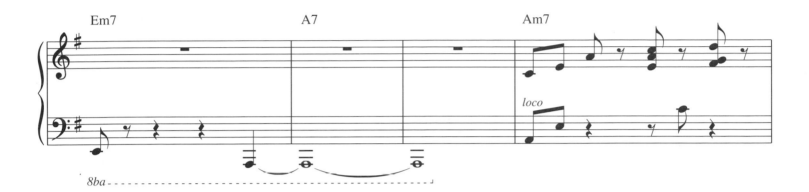

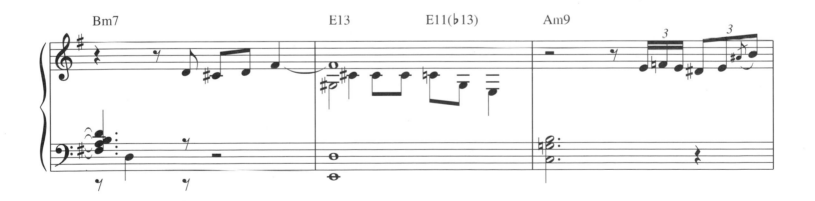

7

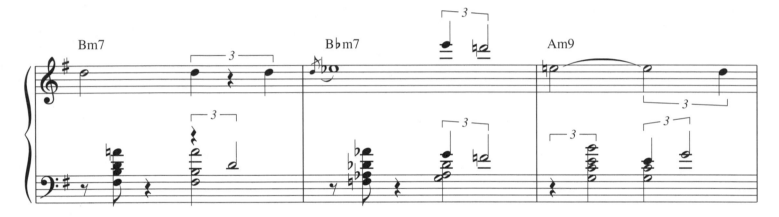

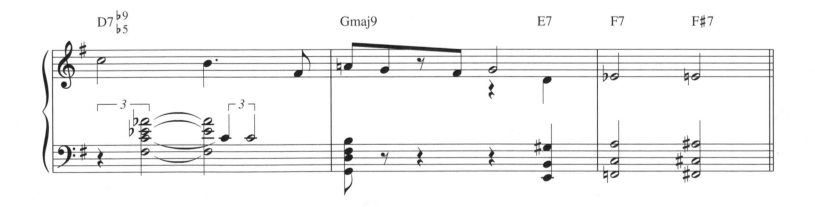

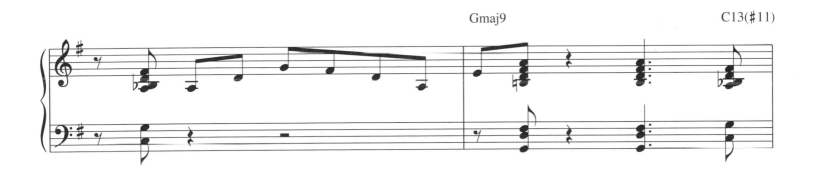

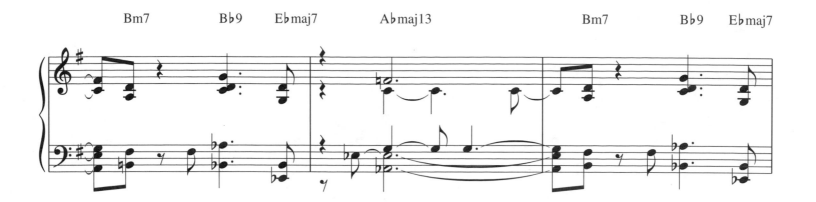

Piano Solo

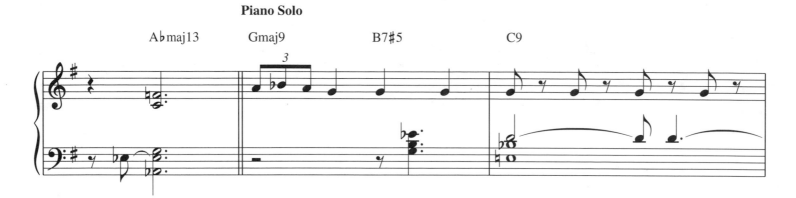

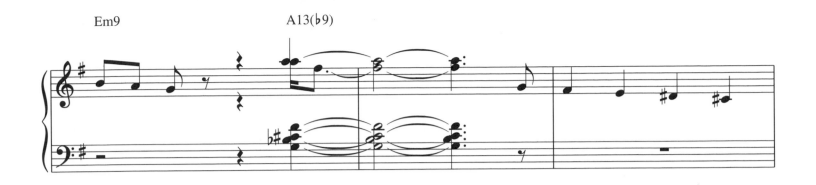

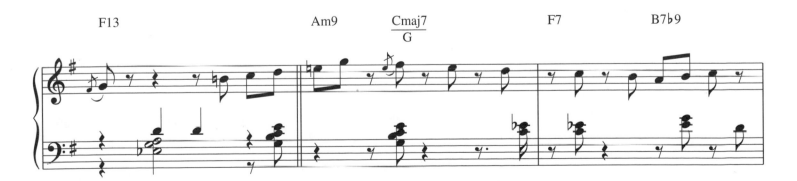

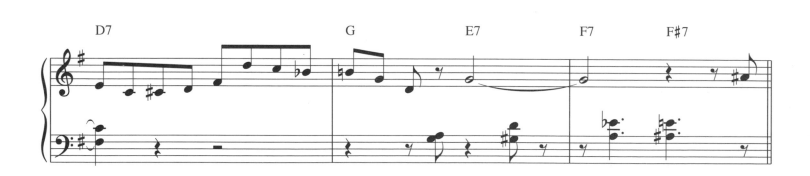

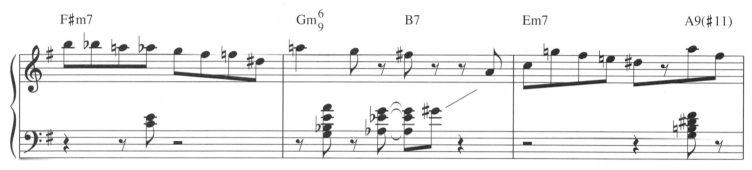

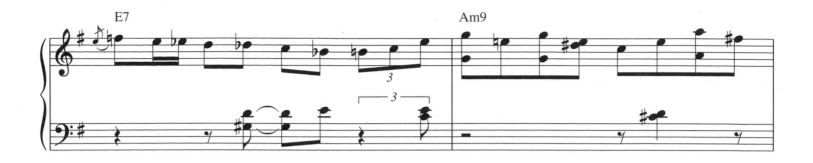

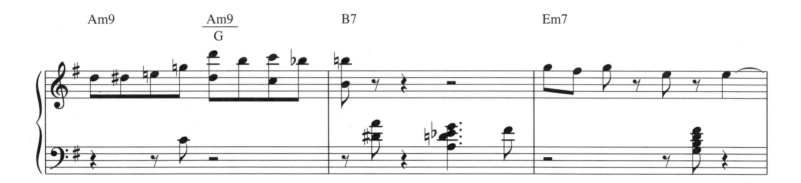

14

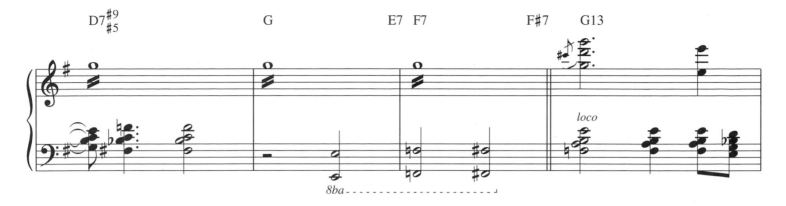

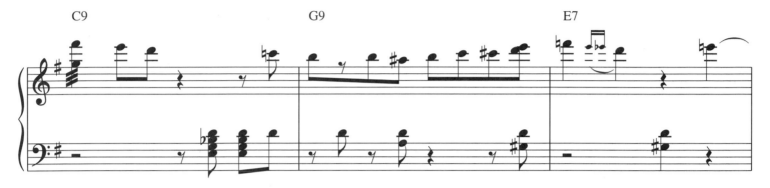

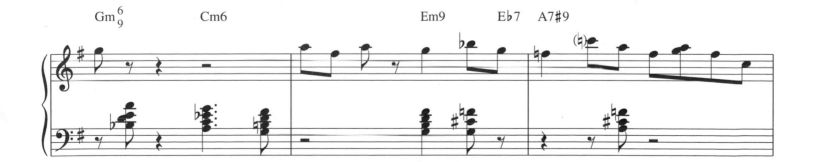

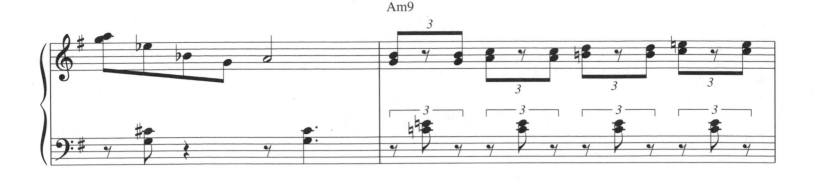

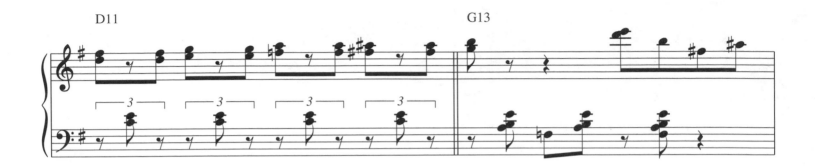

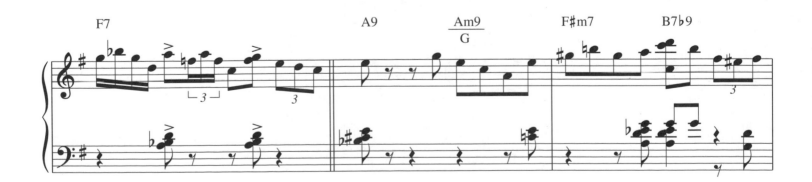

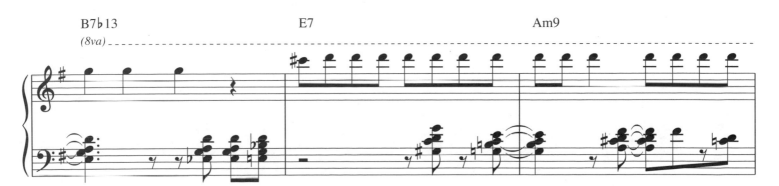

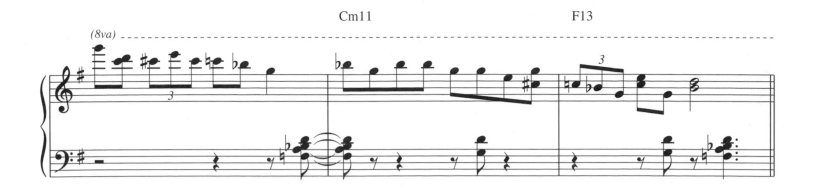

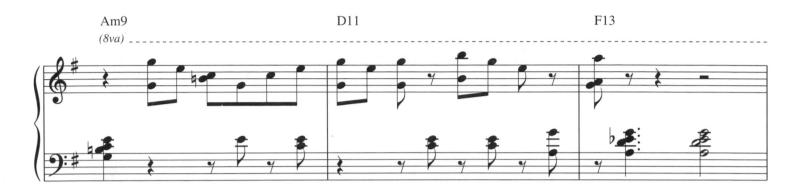

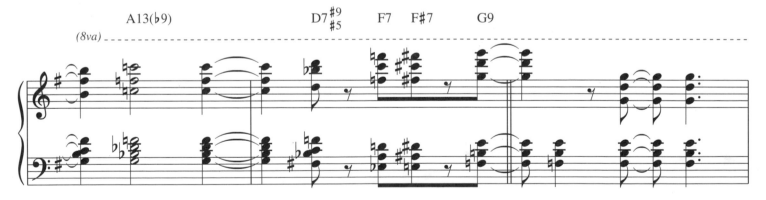

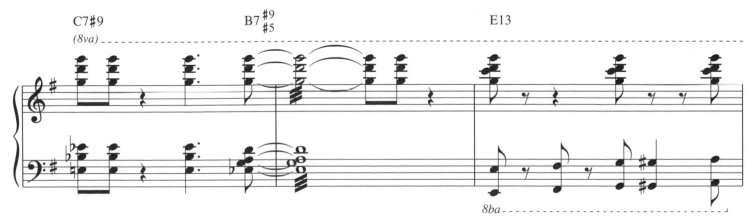

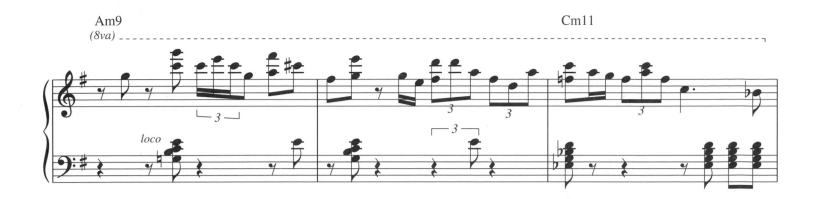

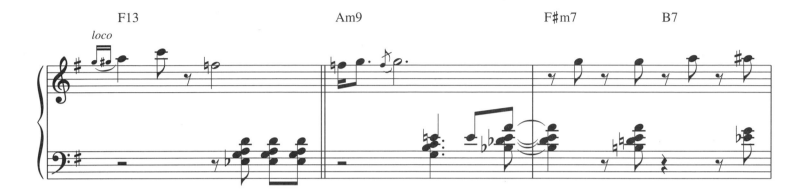

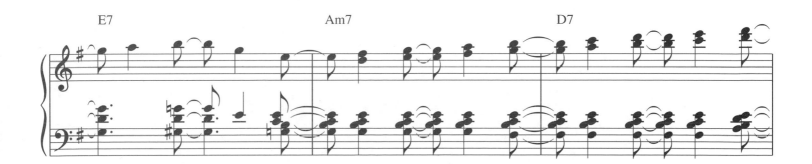

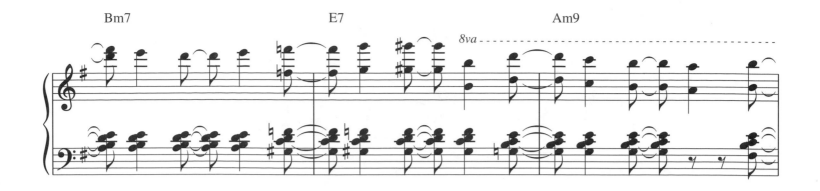

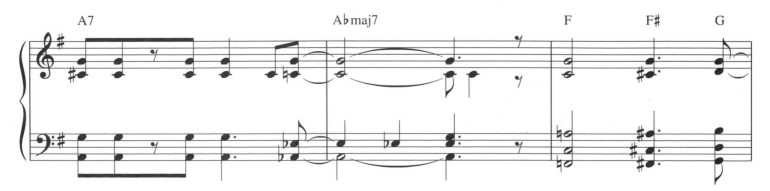

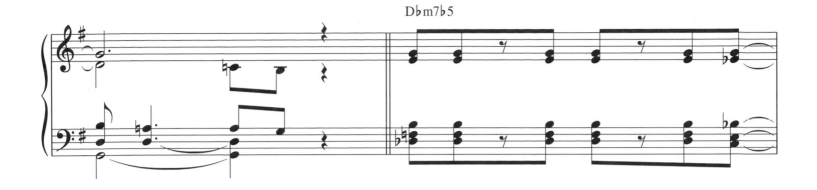

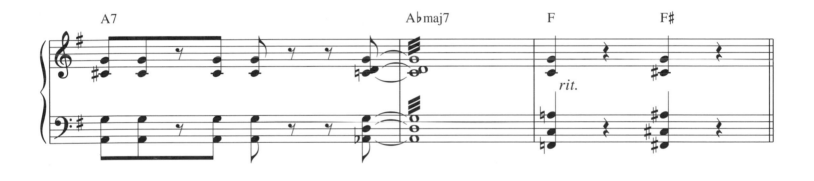

Blue Skies

from *BETSY*

Words and Music by Irving Berlin

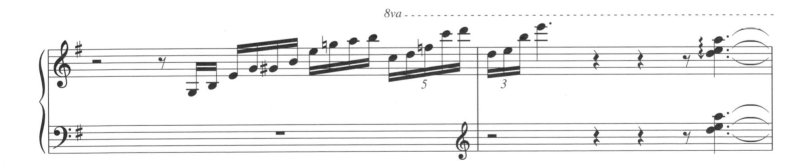

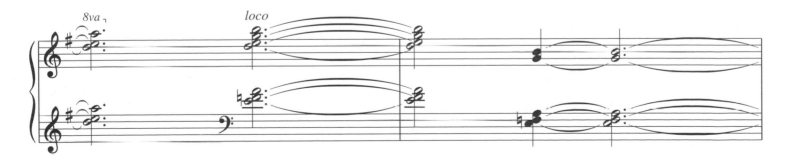

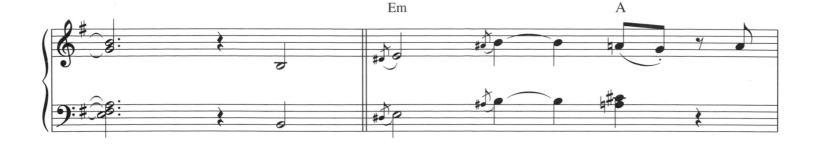

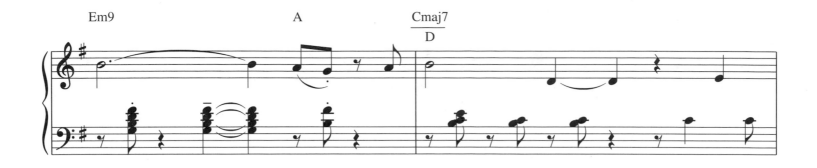

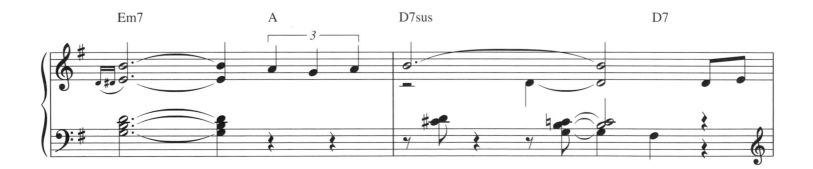

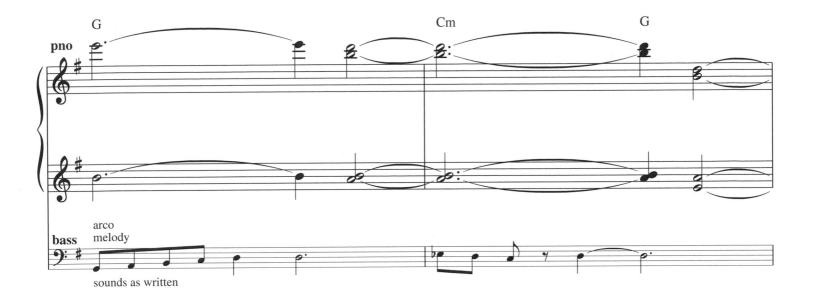

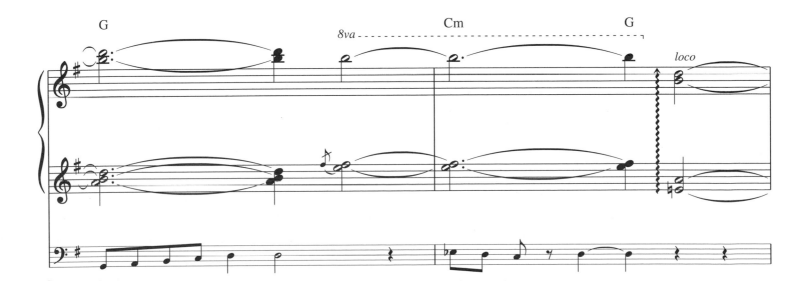

27

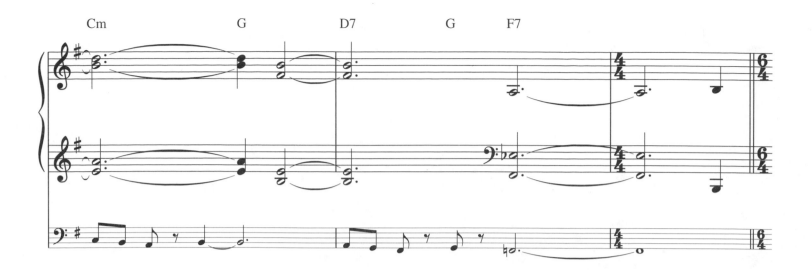

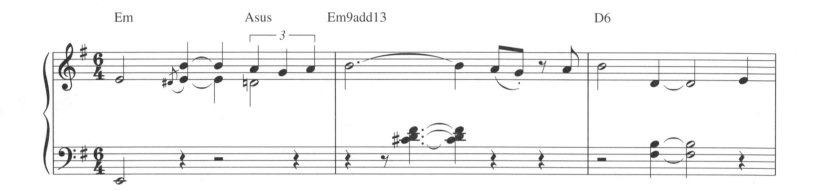

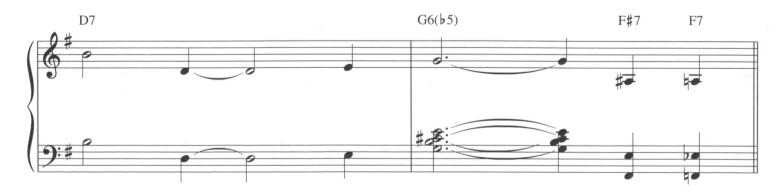

Bass Solo

Piano Solo

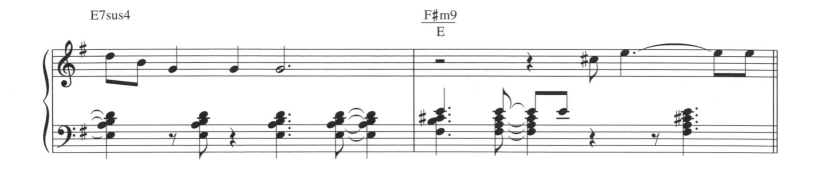

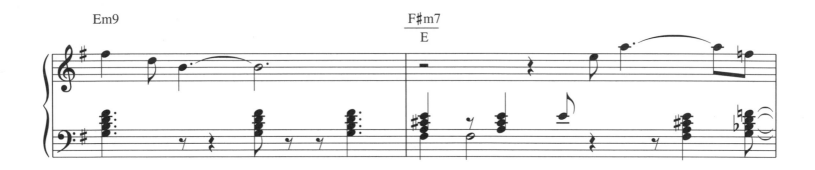

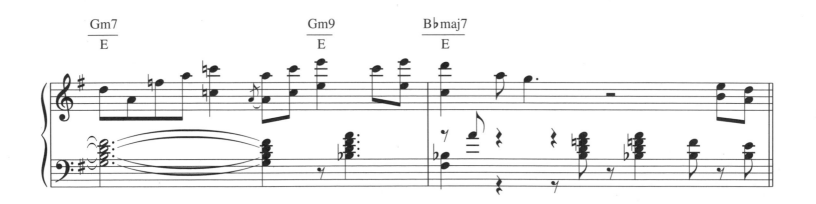

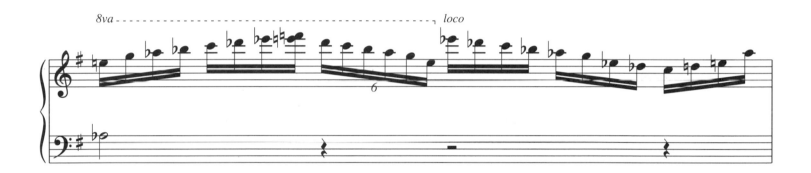

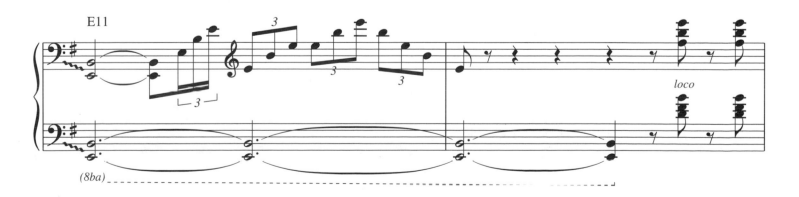

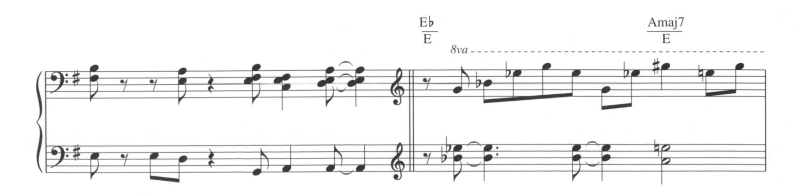

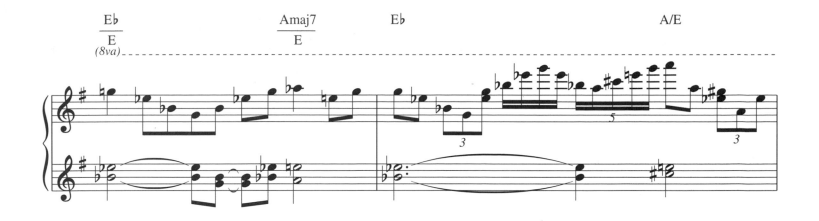

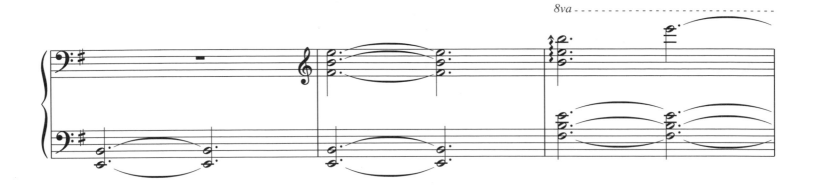

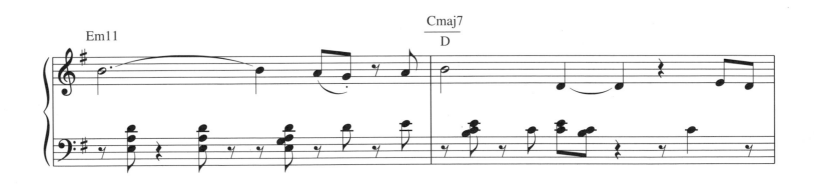

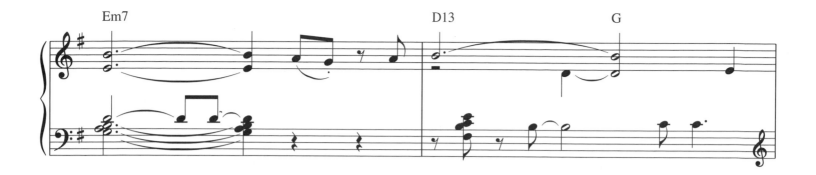

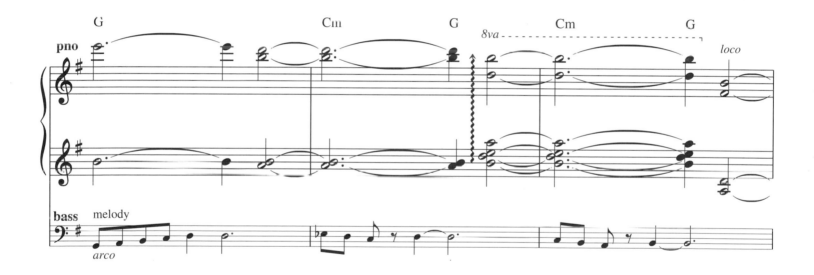

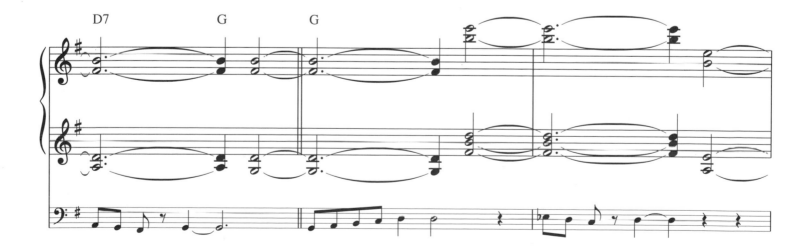

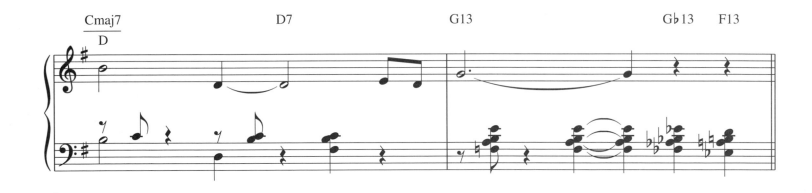

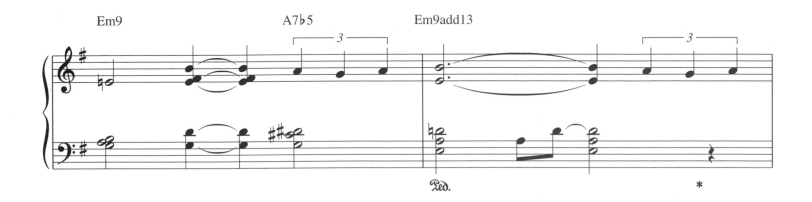

Caravan
from SOPHISTICATED LADIES
Words and Music by Duke Ellington, Irving Mills and Juan Tizol

Intro

B♭m7

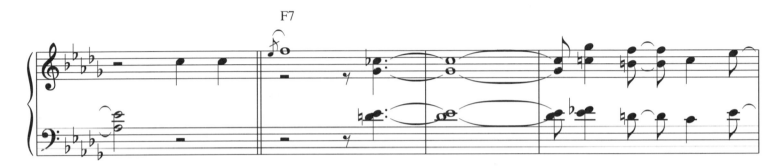

F7

Swing

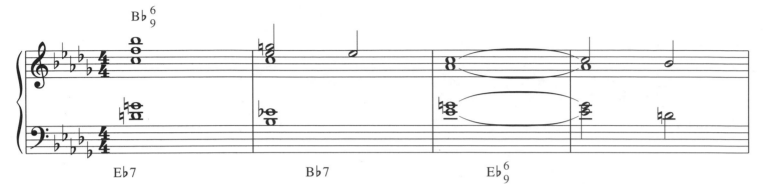

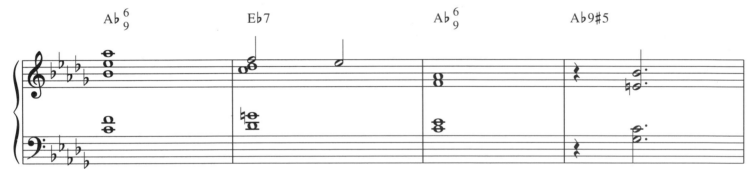

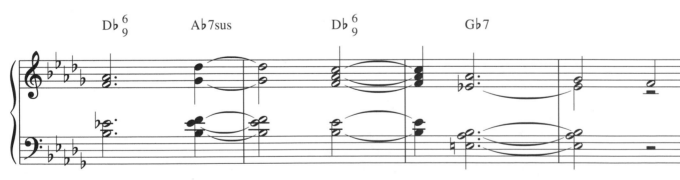

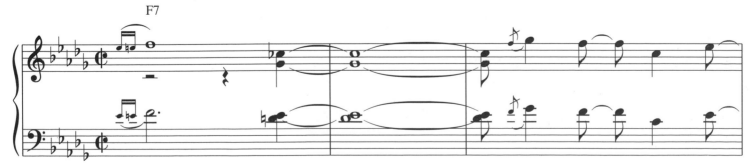

B♭m7

Piano Solo

F7

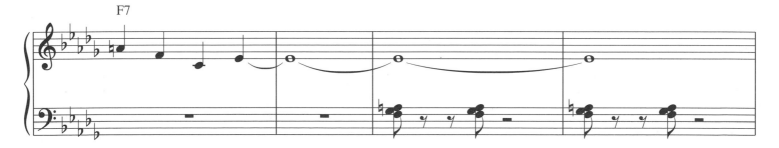

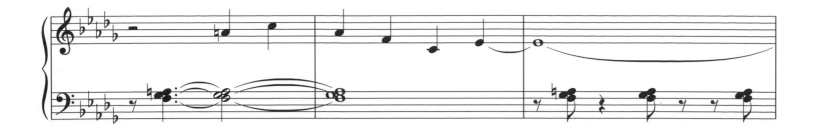

Eb7

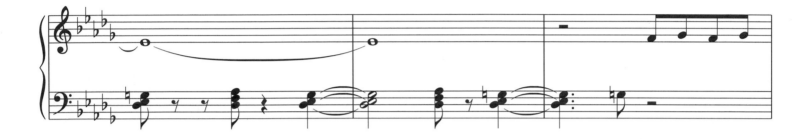

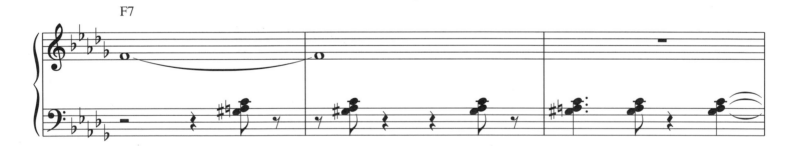

F7

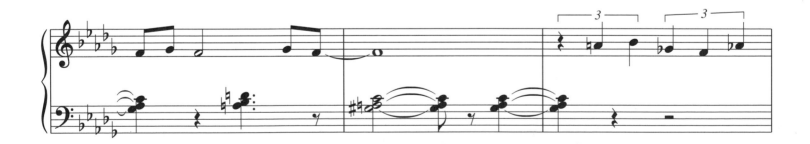

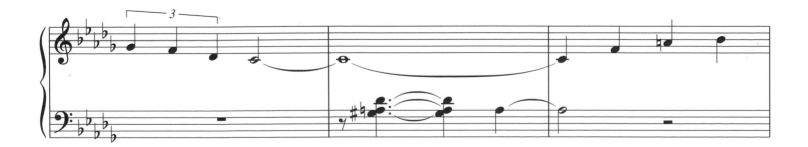

Swing

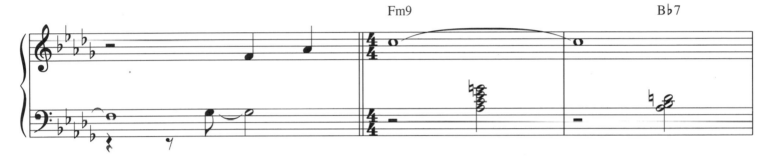

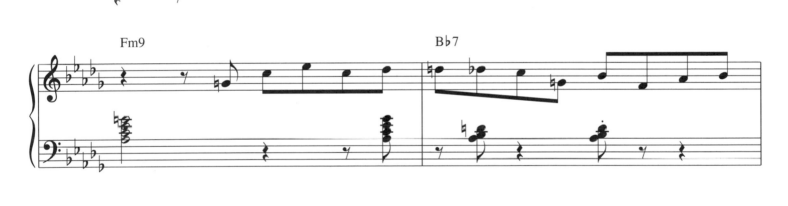

Latin

F7

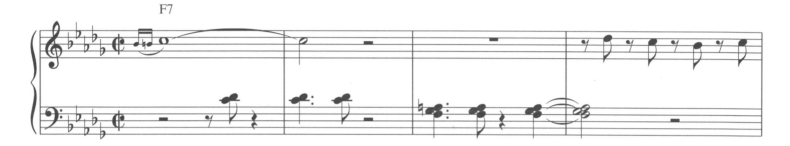

Bbm7

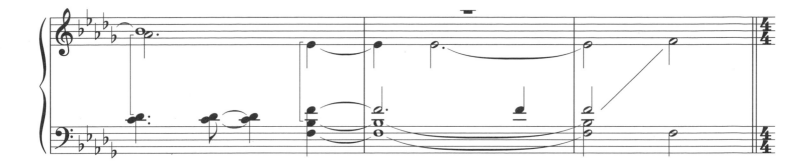

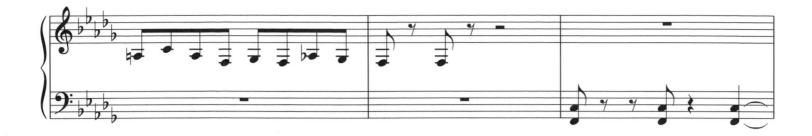

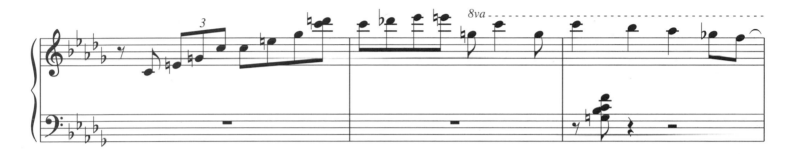

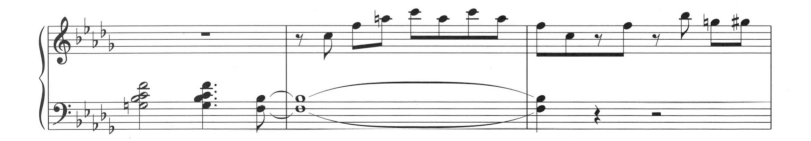

F7

F7

F7

Swing

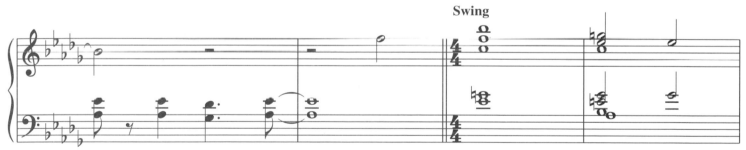

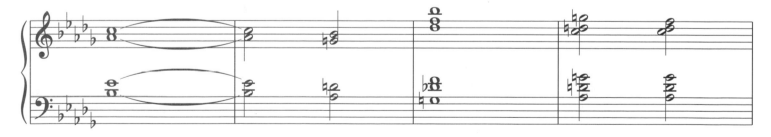

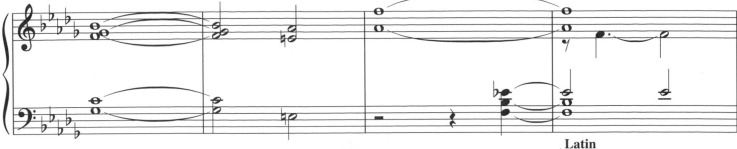

Latin

F7

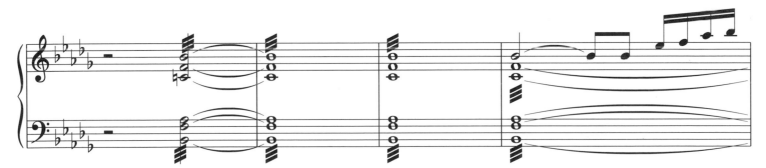

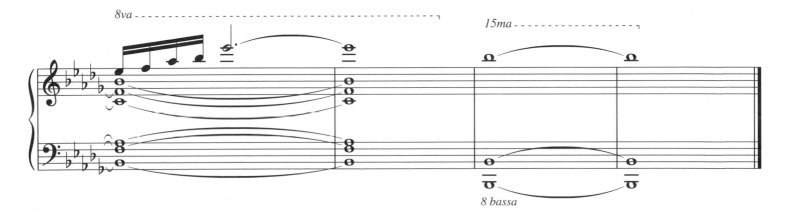

Elegie

By Jules Massenet
Arranged by Cyrus Chestnut

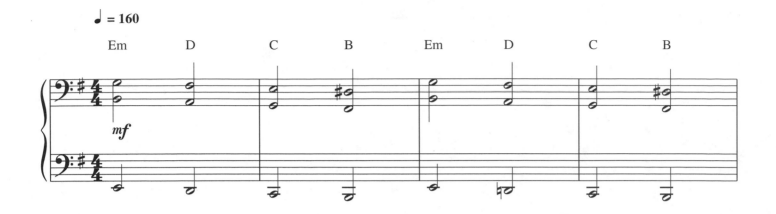

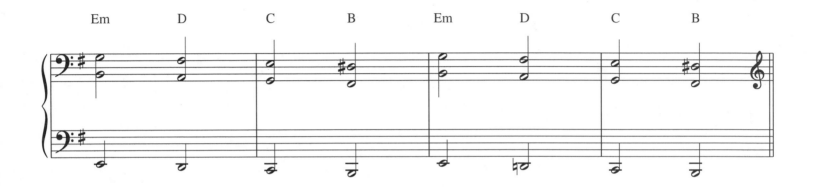

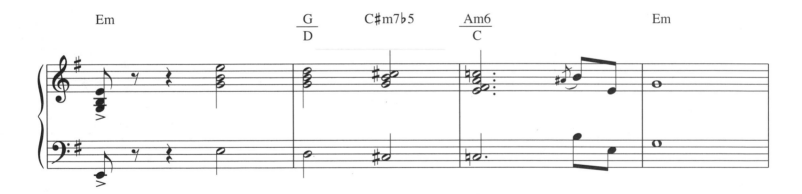

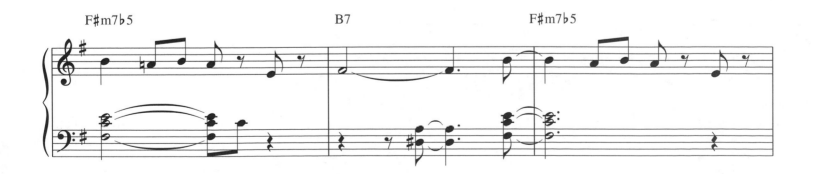

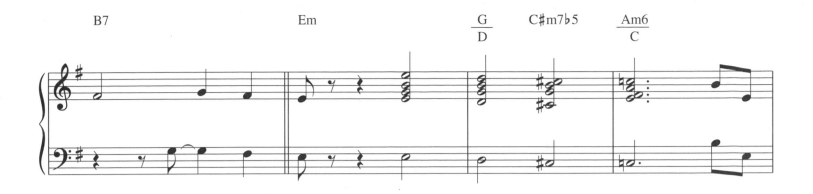

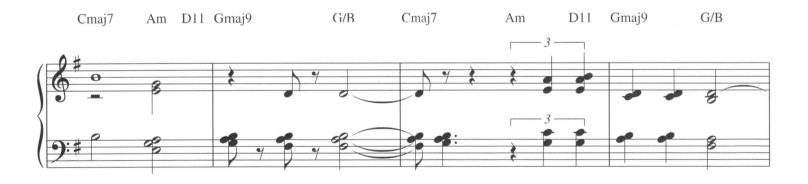

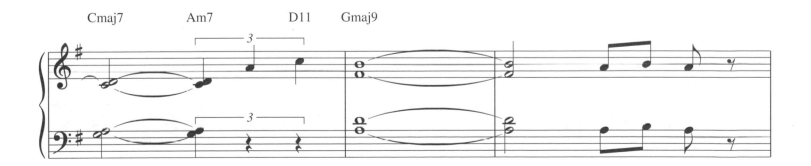

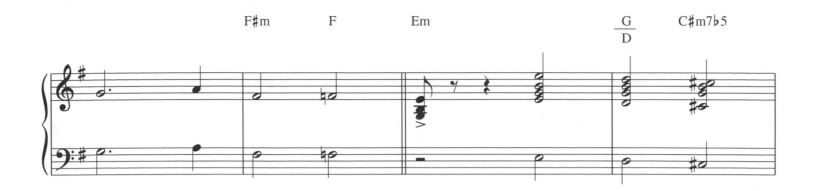

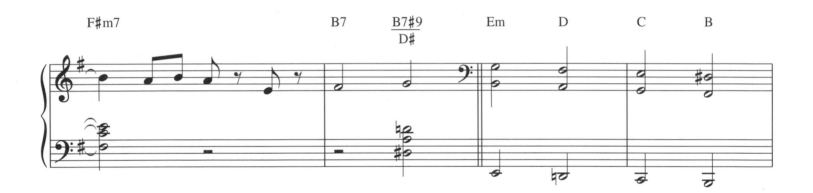

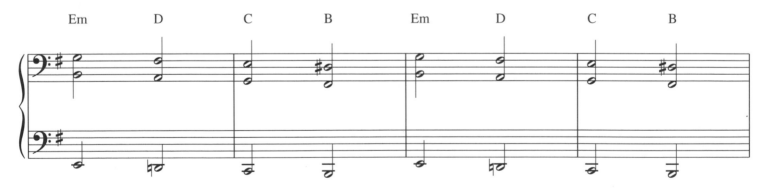

Piano Solo

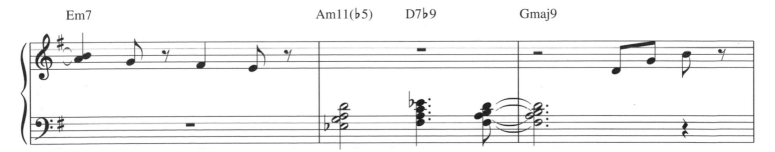

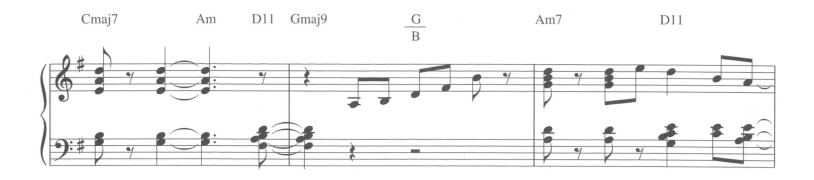

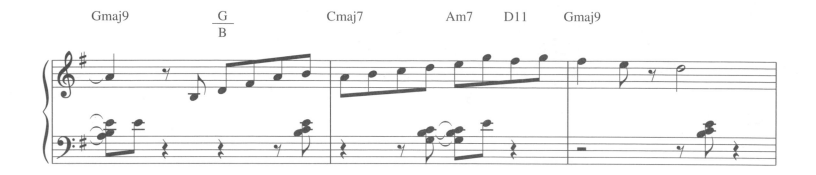

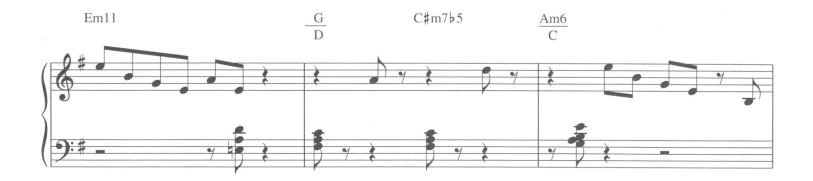

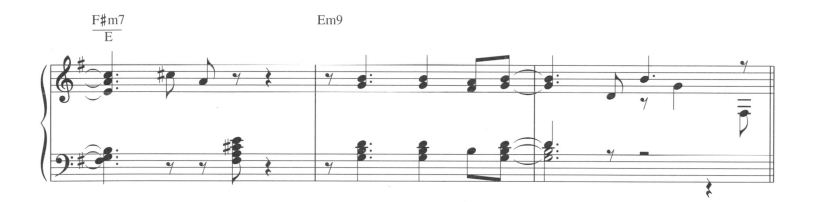

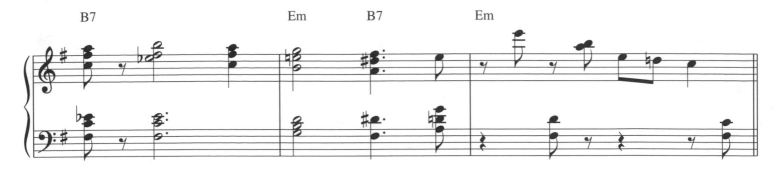

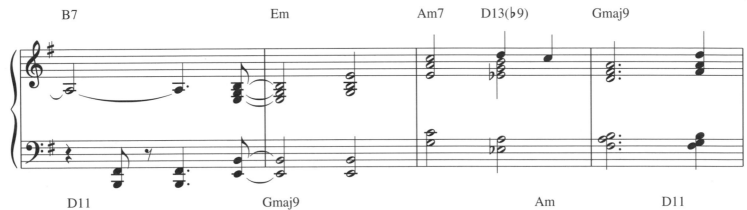

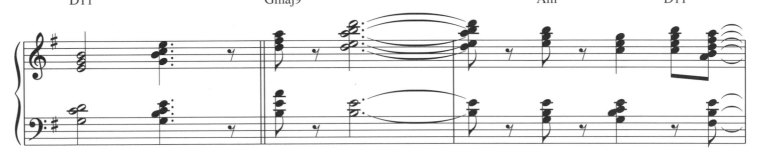

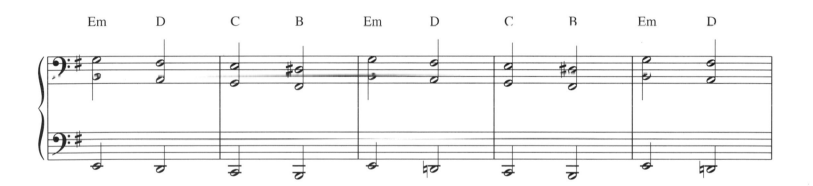

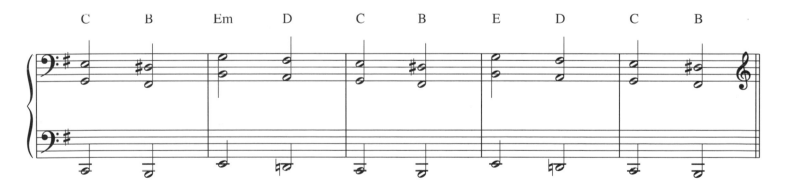

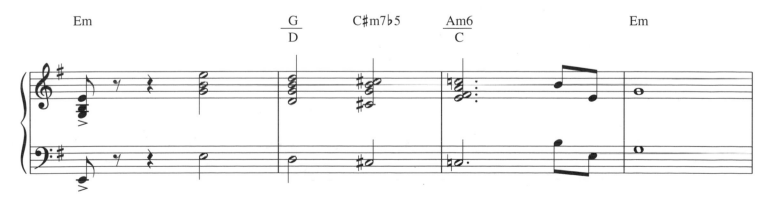

63

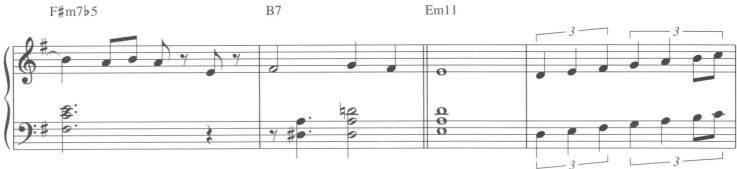

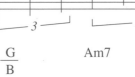

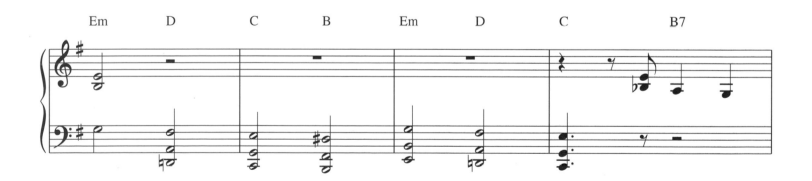

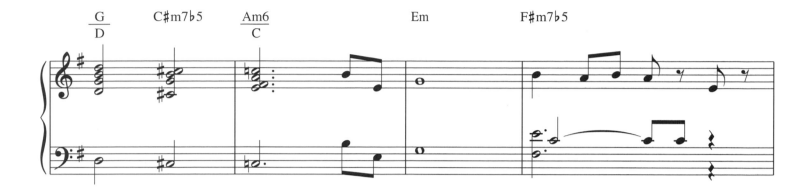

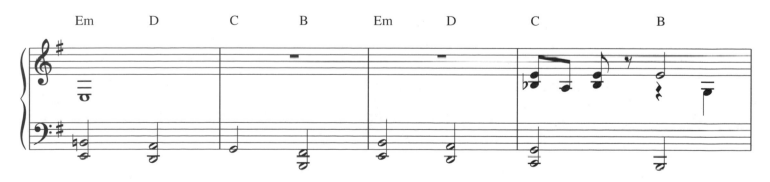

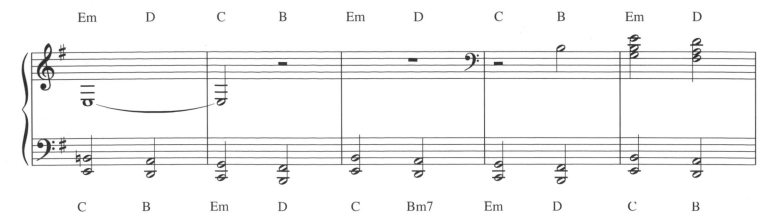

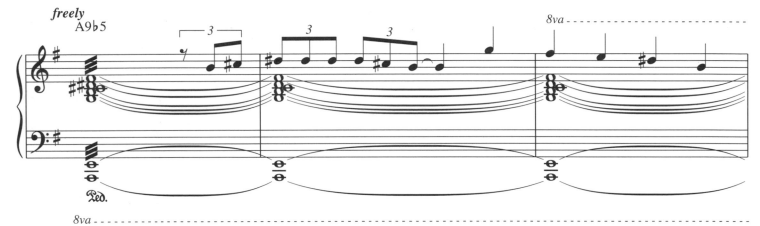

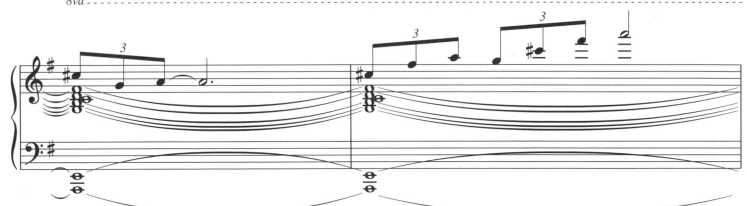

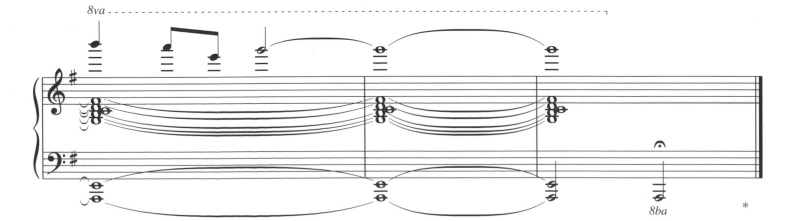

My Funny Valentine

from *BABES IN ARMS*

Words by Lorenz Hart
Music by Richard Rodgers

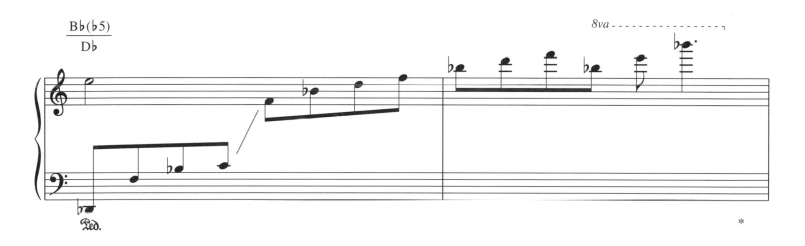

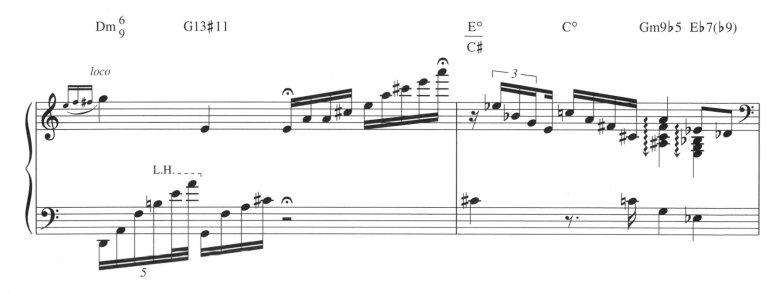

G13/F   Eb7

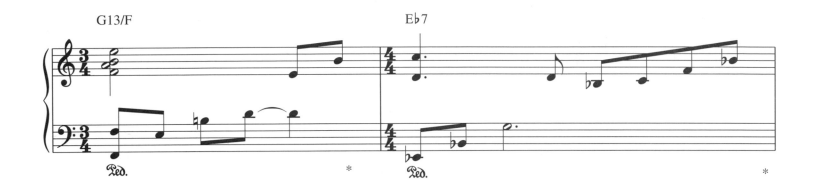

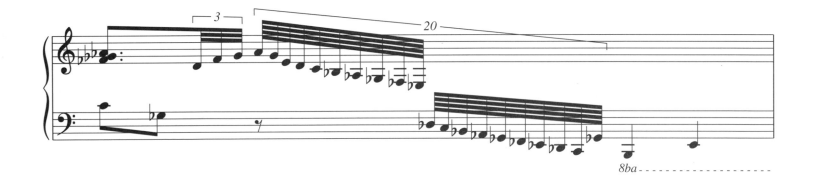

Am9   Fmaj13#11   Am9

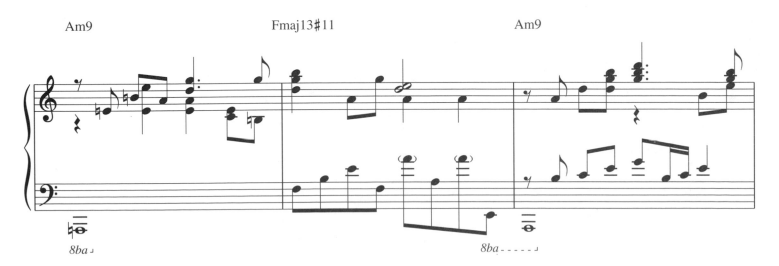

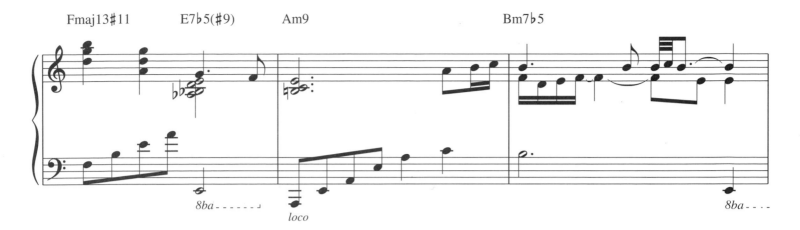

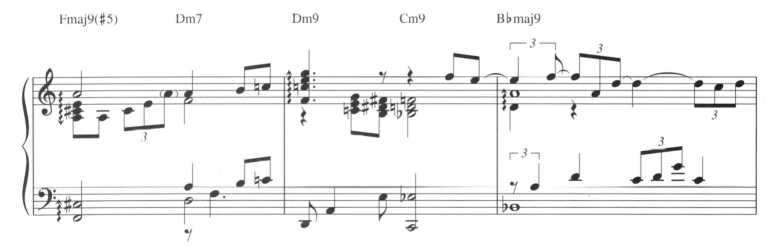

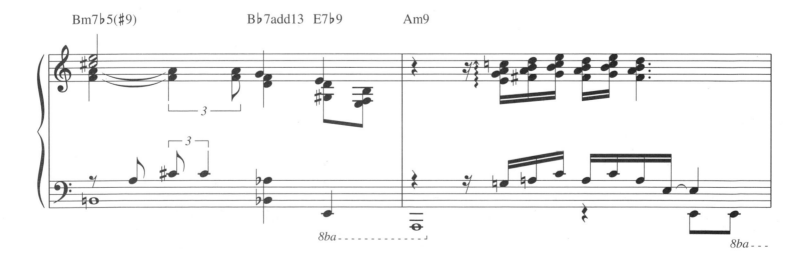

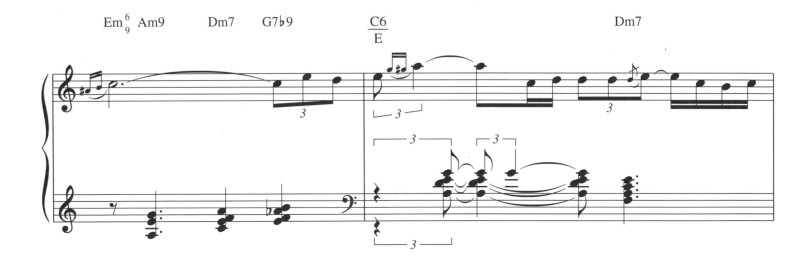

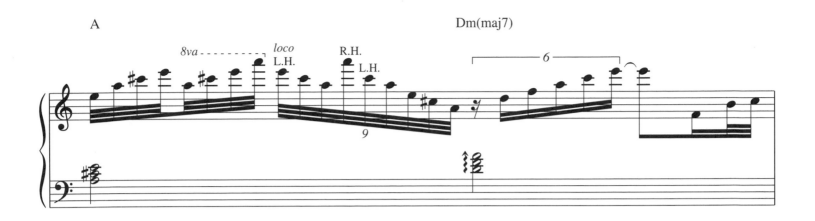

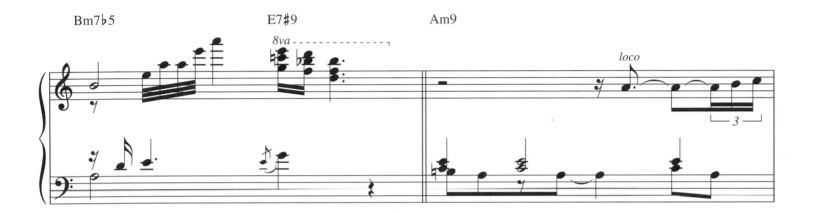

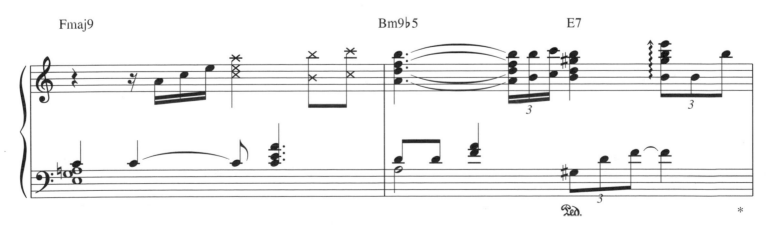

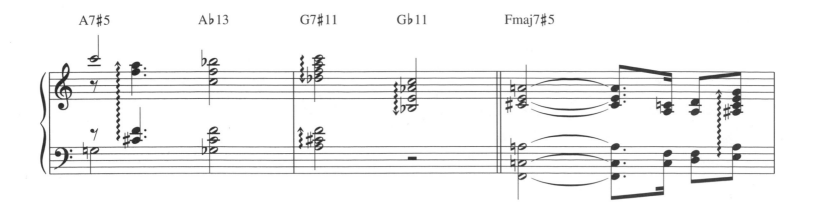

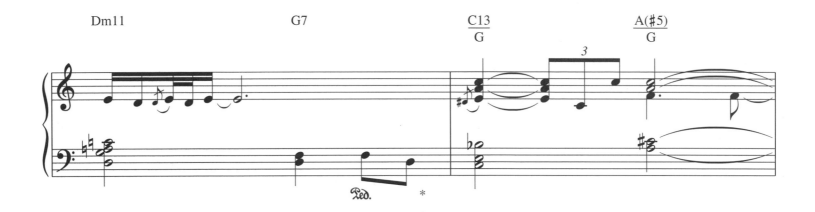

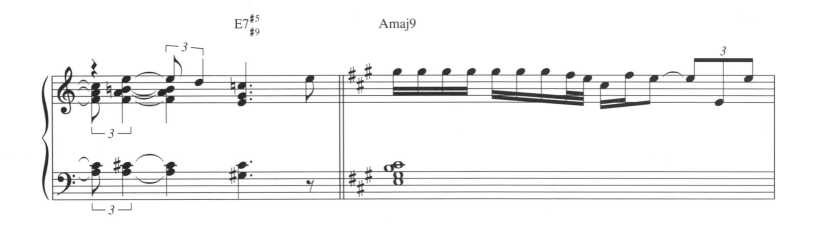

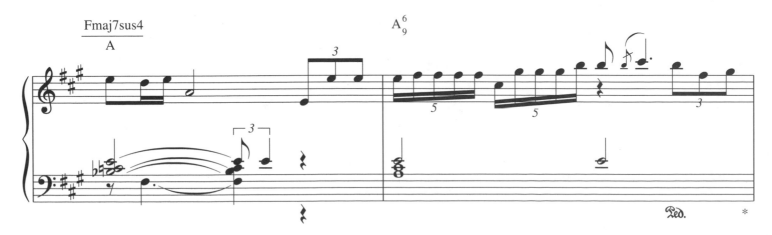

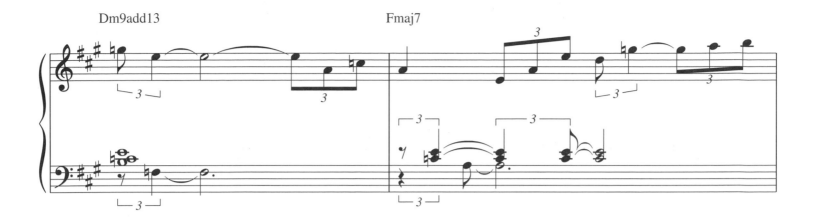

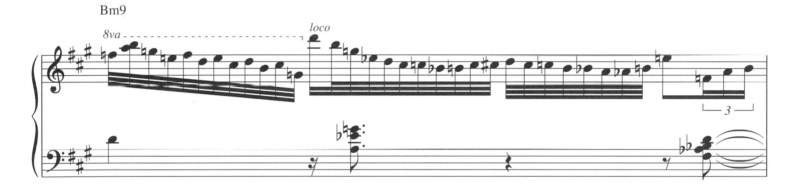

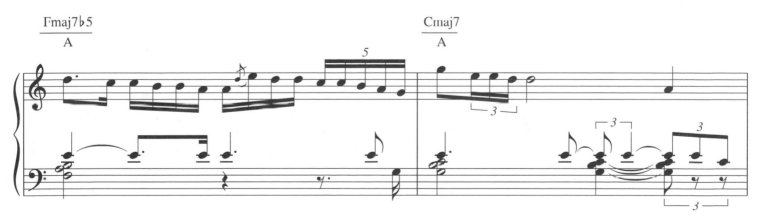

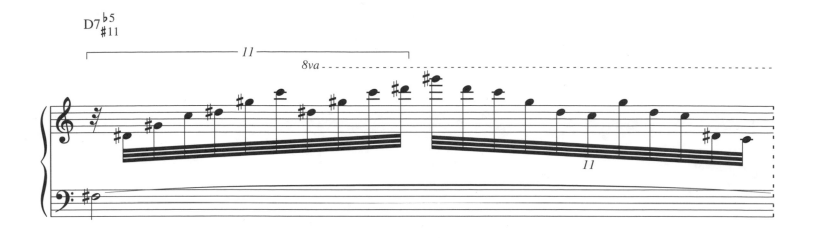

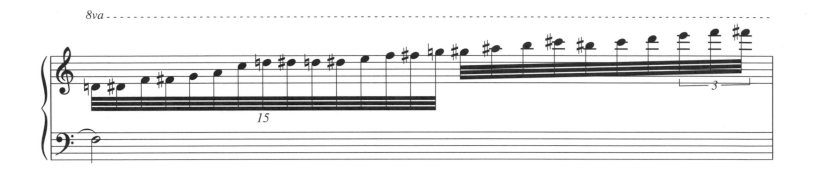

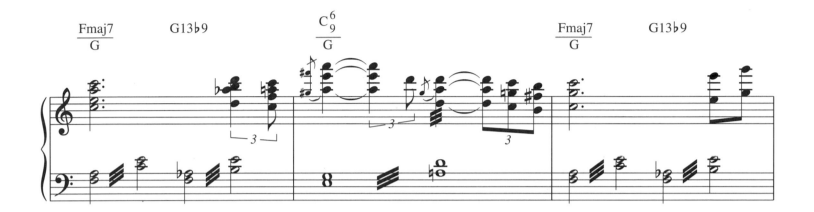

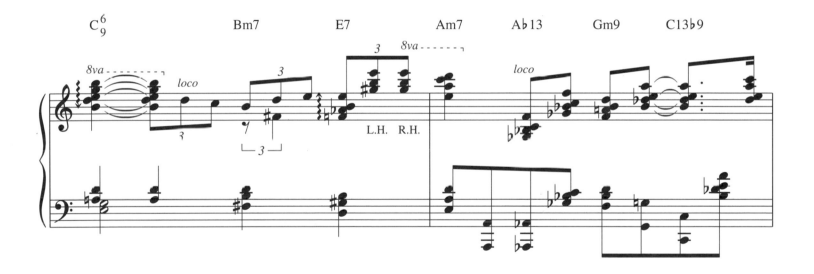

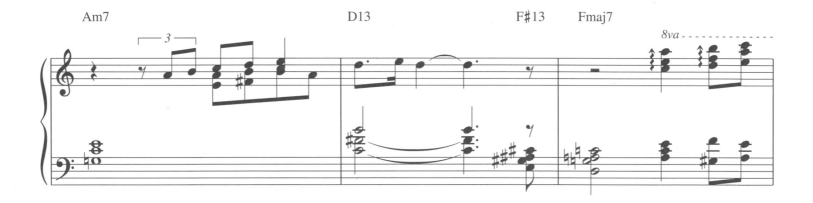

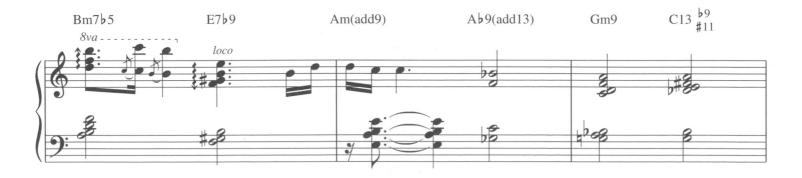

Solo Piano

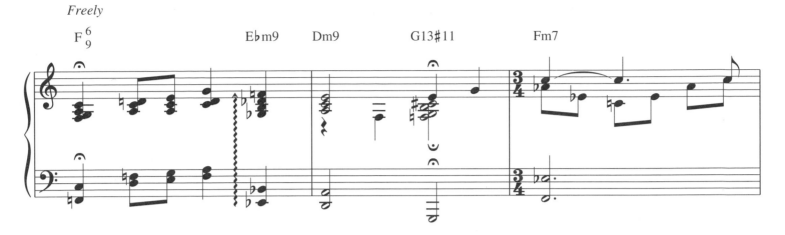

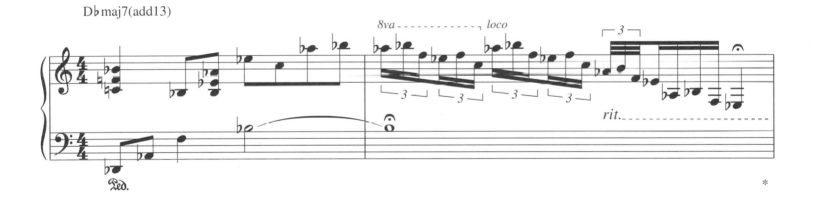

77

Revelation

By Cyrus Chestnut

♩ = 168

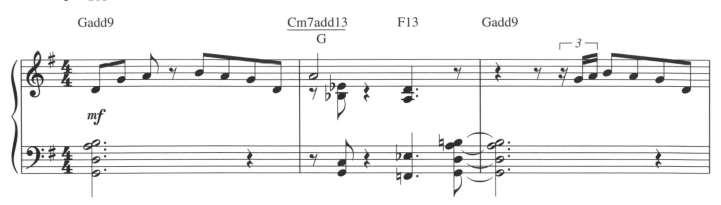

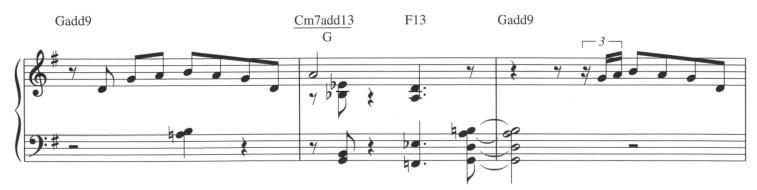

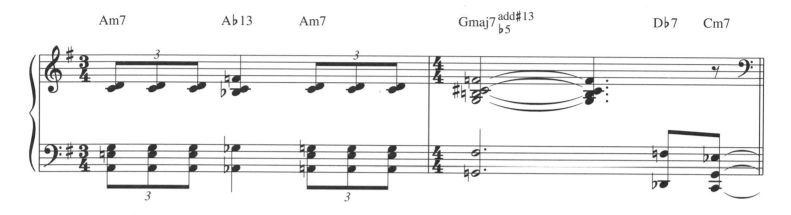

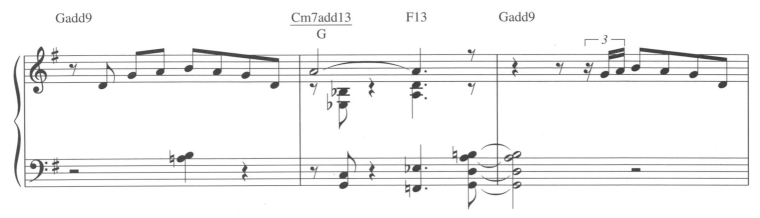

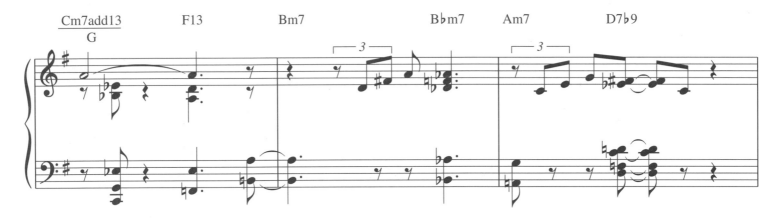

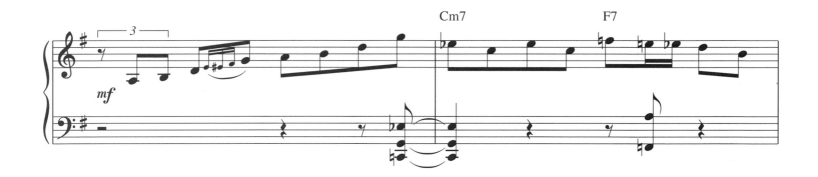

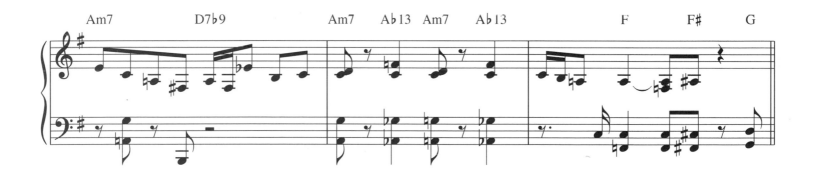

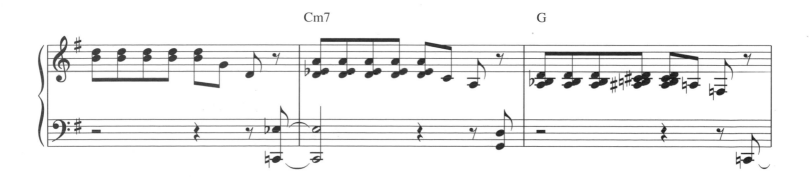

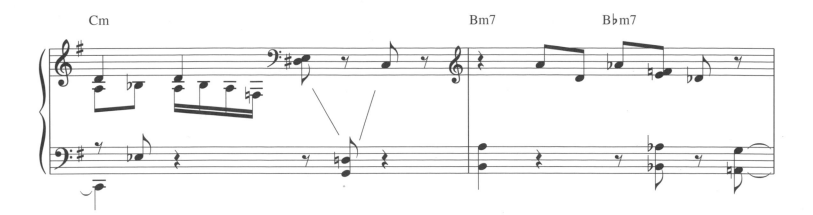

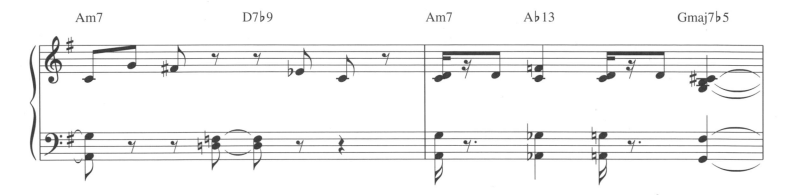

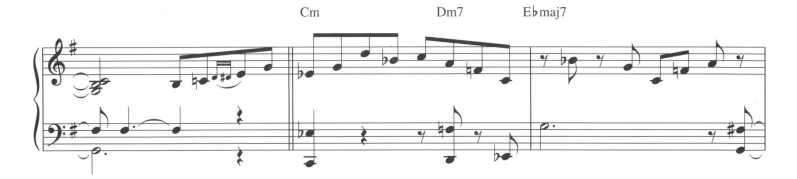

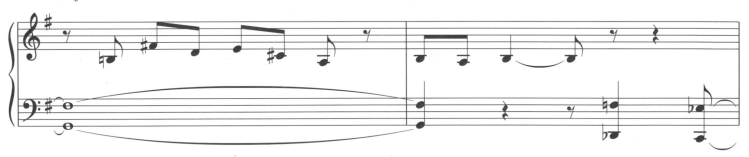

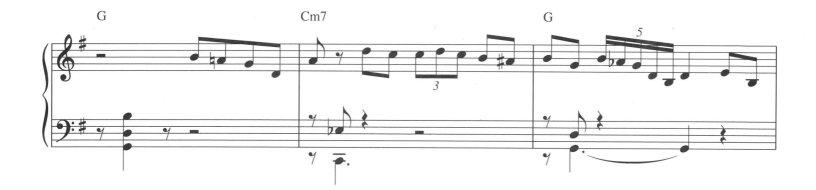

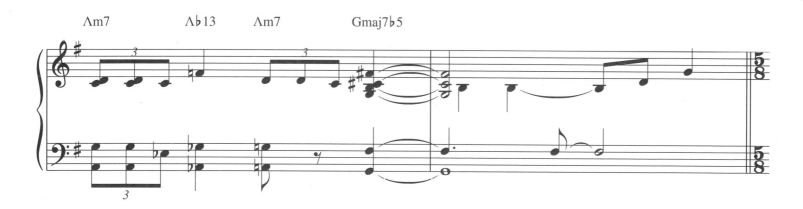

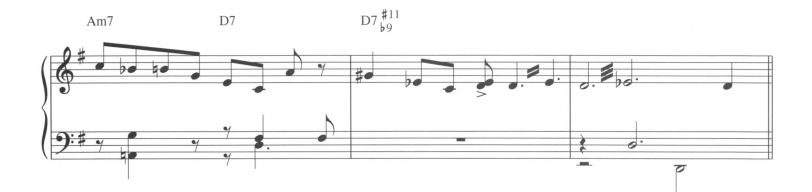

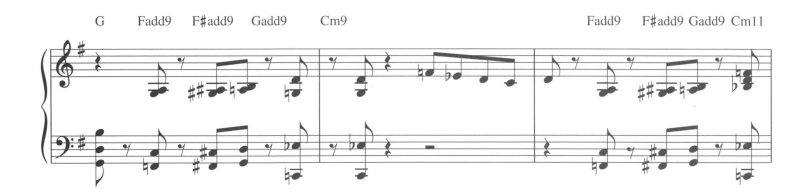

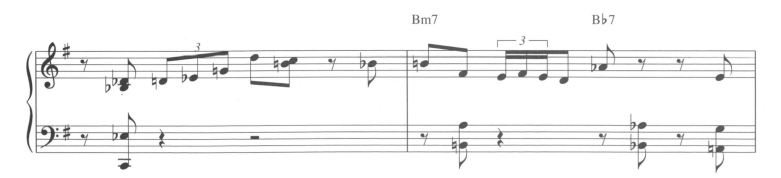

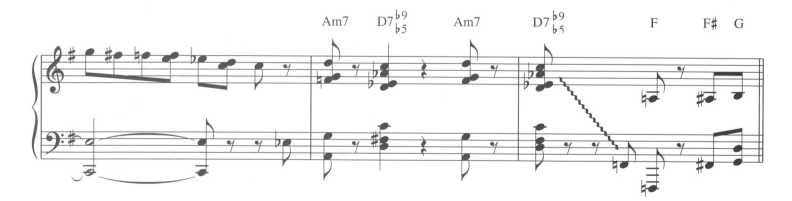

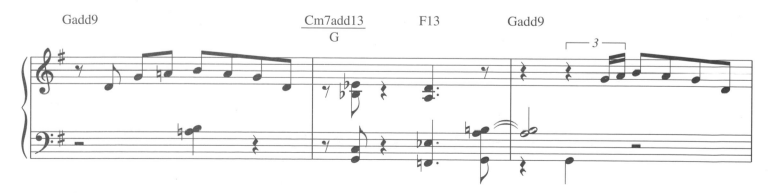

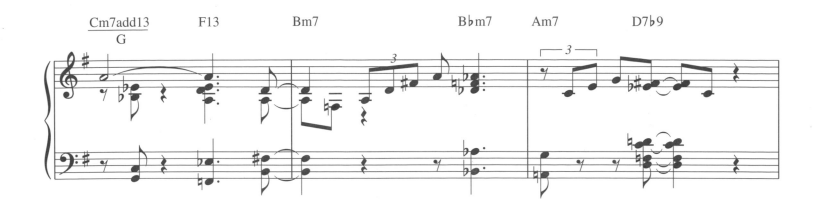

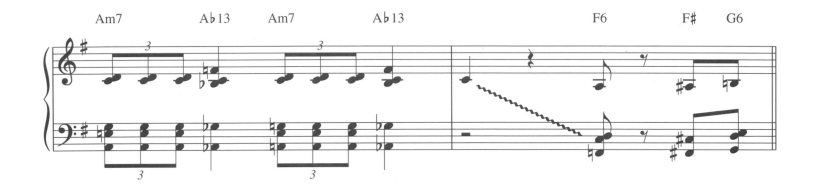

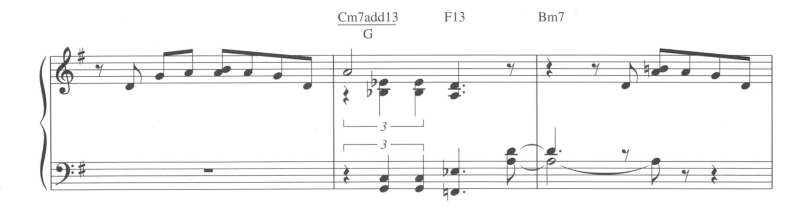

Tenderly

from *TORCH SONG*

Lyric by Jack Lawrence
Music by Walter Gross

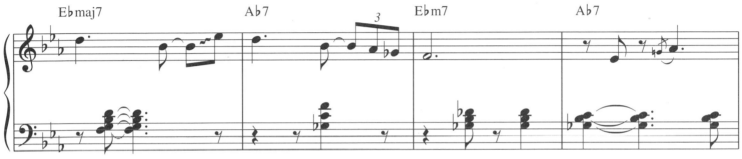

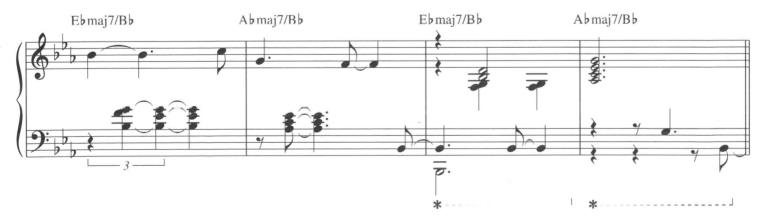

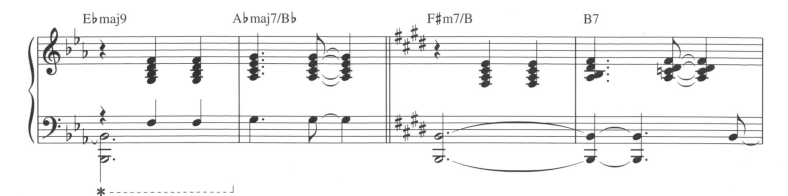

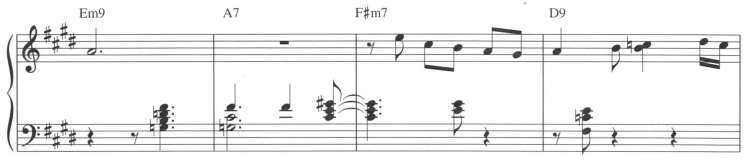

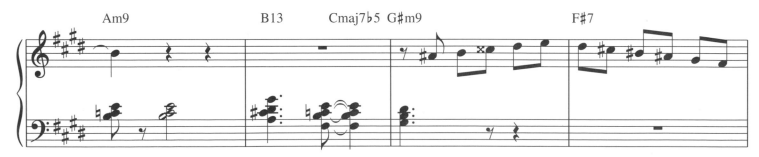

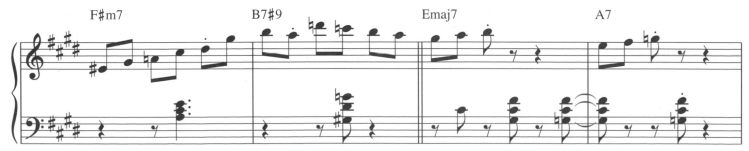

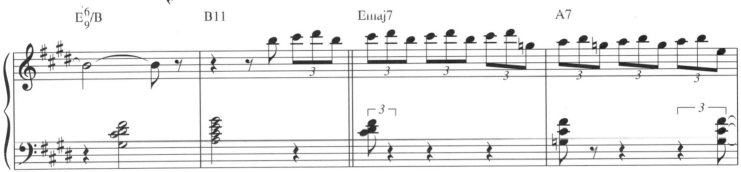

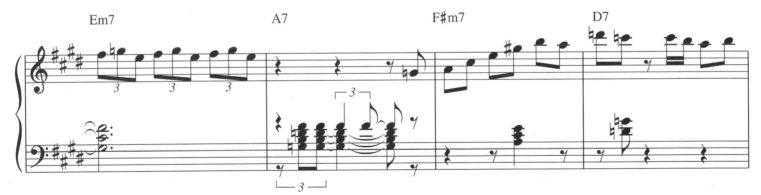

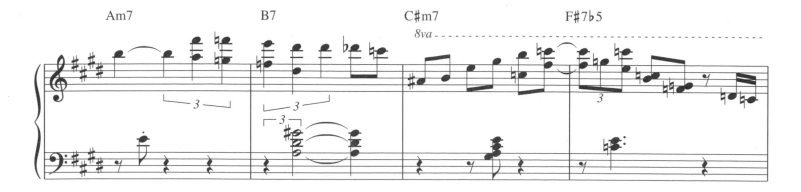

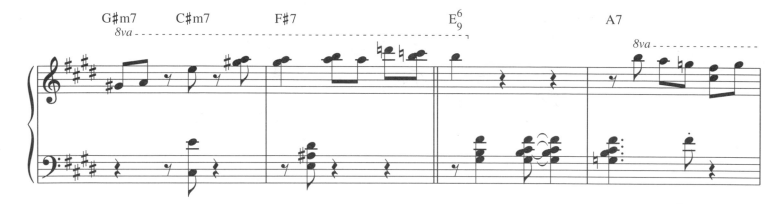

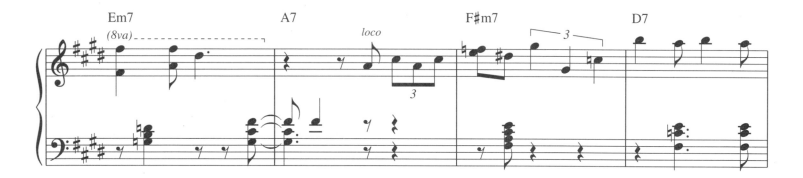

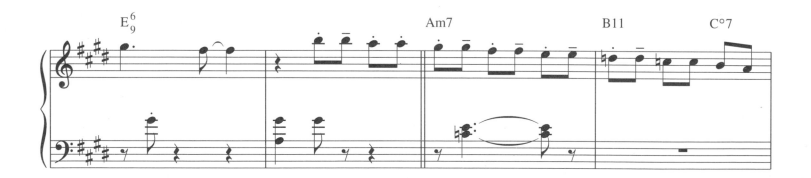

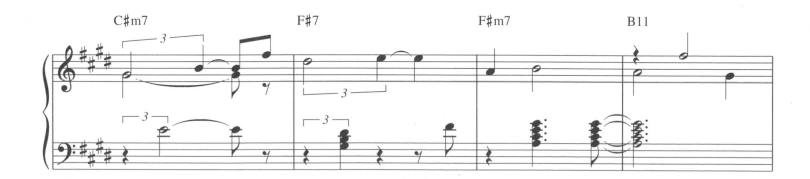

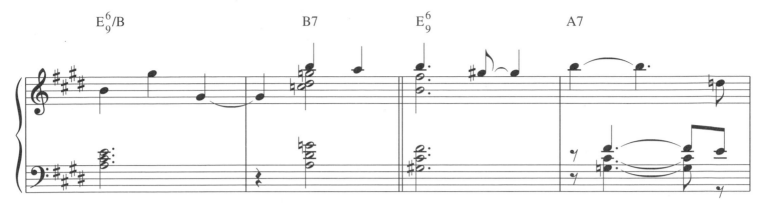

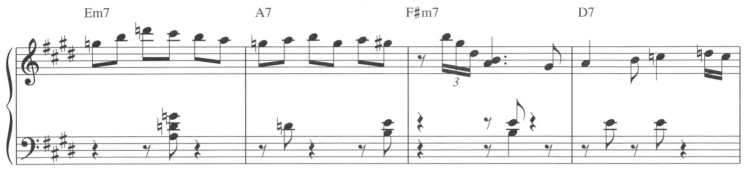

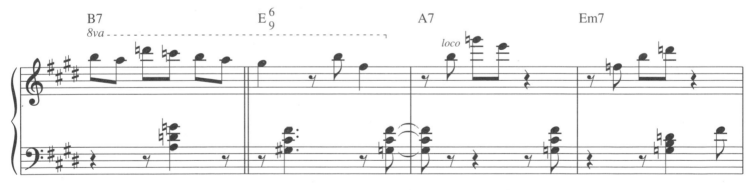

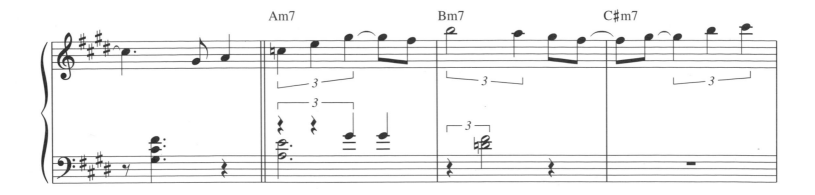

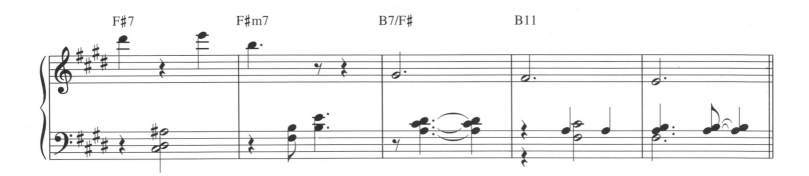

Bass Solo

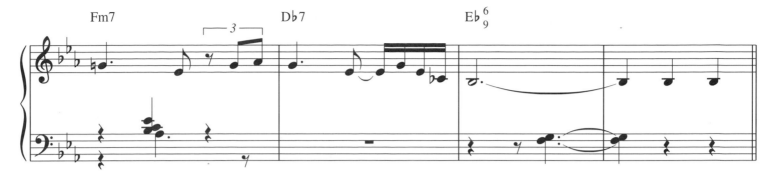

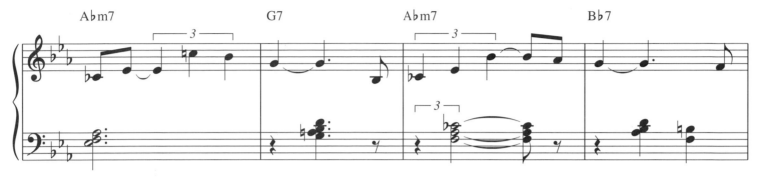

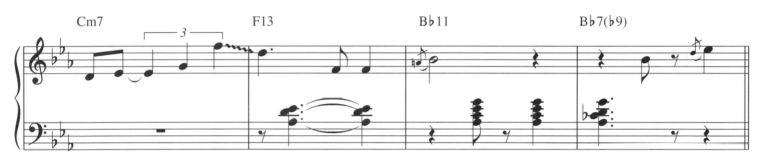

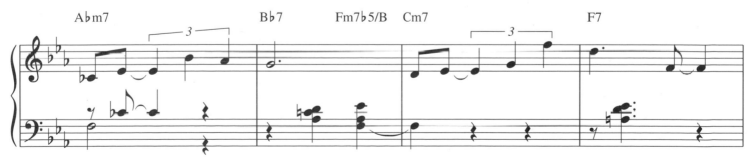

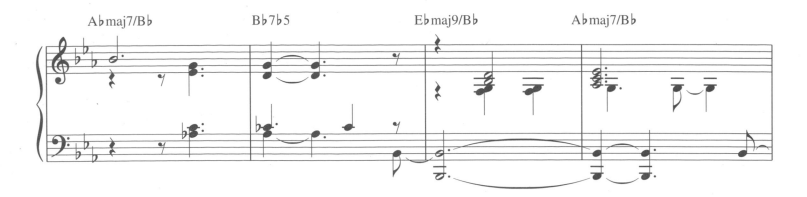

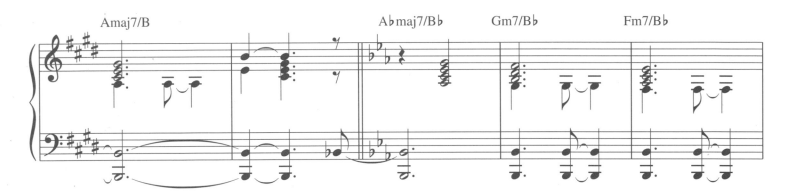